I0186657

demolitions
and
reconstructions

demolitions
and
reconstructions

jacob erin-cilberto

demolitions and reconstructions
Copyright © 2015 jacob erin-cilberto
All Rights Reserved

No part of this publication may be reproduced, stored in a
retrieval system or transmitted in any form or by any means,
electronic, mechanical, photocopying, recording or
otherwise, without the prior written permission of both the
copyright owner and the publisher of this book.

ISBN-13: 978-0692409183
ISBN-10: 0692409181

Published by Water Forest Press
PO Box 295, Stormville, NY 12582
WaterForestPress.com

Layout & Design by V.R. Valentine
Edited by P. Valentine

Cover Art © Welcomia (Dreamstime)

Printed in the United States of America

"Out there in the dark
There's a beckoning candle, yeah

And while I can think, while I can talk
While I can stand, while I can walk
While I can dream, oh, please let my dream
Come true, ohh, right now
Let it come true right now, ohh, yeah"   (Walter Earl Brown)

for all those who dreamed
and still dream of peace and love...

Several of these poems appeared in the following magazines:

New York Dreaming
Voices on the Wind
Expressions
Rivers of Blue Poetry
Leaves of Ink
Smashed Cat
Rib Cage
Atherton Review
Miracle Magazine
Ginosko Anthology #2
Cyclamens and Swords
The River Muse
Torrid Literature
Poem and Poetry
Fluid Writer
Distilled Lives (Volume 2)

Titles in this Collection

this poem is not about poets

they get too much attention already
with their metaphorically mixed up minds
and their senile simile similarities

everything is poets poets poets
lascivious laureates
and their laboring over so many lines
sweating over each syllable
so what?

i sweat,
i labor
i'm similar to others
just a normal nomad traveling through books
of rhyme
spending too much time
paying attention to poets

who write prolific pontificates
dogmatic doggerels
diatribes to be noteworthy nexuses

to a literary world
that already pays too much attention
to poets while their plebeian
counterparts

co-exist with so little fanfare
that it's totally unfair—
so i shall reiterate what i so vehemently indicate
so irately

this poem is not about poets

rolling down the foggy window of youth

i loved you a thousand times
in the back seat of my '66
olds-mind

that radio played into the moonlight
and those quarter moon kisses
melted me into the cushion

as i braced against your becoming
we shed bras,blouses, belts
and restless needs

absorbed into rock and roll logic
and then the soft melodies skimmed the waves
we sailed into the oblivion that was teen intensity

then you whispered in my ear
as i felt your breath formulate words
i would never again not hear

because they were forever etched
into the yearbook of my heart
scribblings of unidentified secrets

only you and i held
as we grabbed on tighter
and i started the engine

that brought us home.

There was a Time

what did you see?
when your eyes still saw happenstance
among circumstance
but reason left you,
when nothing made sense anymore
except the sense that nothing was there

except weeks, or days
of sand emptying from the hour glass mind

the tilting of history
so many years written into a life
a backlog of dreams waiting to prosper
fantasies committed to fruition
but the tuition invalid
the checks never balanced enough
to warrant coming true,
not all of them,
but already enough had played out
and you danced within them

closed your eyes and believed in what there was
what there could be
what you saw in him,

and you lived with that sense of engagement—
passion,
day-to-day exhilaration even for the simplest of things
even the mundane having meaning,

and then you closed your eyes one more time
dreams drifted just out of reach
sense, their companion,

and love,
it just kept sleeping.

The Older they Wear

an old poem
fell out of the cuff
of my blue jeans
discolored, full of sand
from that walk on the beach
the last time i saw you

i carved your name into the first few lines
and sat under their shade
dreaming of beached love
wondering why we couldn't surface closer to a shore
that would keep us together

an old poem
fell out of my shirt pocket
as i was pulling the memory of you over my head
undressing the feelings, trying on a new wardrobe
but you just kept showing up
like a lint bloom
that won't let a flower grow away from it

so i brought my heart to goodwill
and exchanged it for some used clothes.

warm earth lies just below the cold

plant me in a ground of semblance
so that like the rose
i may rise in blood red petals
of sense,
the past thorns evicted
my youthful convictions
revisited
as the garden's heart
grows toward a new sky

and blue is only a word behind a cloud
as sadness flows out of old wounds
only to saturate the ground
with a drink of rhetoric
to reflower the present
deflower the past

and let me feel the love
that hides in plain sight
between the curvature
of a once befuddled blossom.

jacob erin-cilberto

No Big Wedding Here

two poems eloped
everyone warned it wouldn't work

one was raised with strict
rhyme and reason
metered parents who disapproved
and called their love lesion

because the other was free-verse
written with reckless abandon
raised for theme
to be a Beat's dream
but a purist's nightmare

metaphors fall in love
regardless of race, religion or poetic style
and sometimes have to be read off into the sunset
with a sneer

because others look down their noses
if the poems aren't traditional verses
about roses
and pretty trees
and clouds and sunshine

but this poem's love was none of the above
it was about America screwing itself as a nation
about love failing
about hearts ailing
and it had no pretty wrapping
and no black ribbon tapping
of perfect alliteration

just blank envy from its peers
editing red faces
and jeers

and "how could you's?"
from readers with iambic ire
and prejudicial fire

mired in their own bias
thinking so inside the box
they couldn't see

the perfect union
that could be
as you and me
became

two poems eloped
sharing very different verses
quite eloquently.

jacob erin-cilberto

Was Long Ago, but not

tomorrow is fast approaching
and once again my reflection
will burn with thoughts of you

your soft eyes in candlelit
dreams, haunting me
with a touch that houses

the strumming of my heart
your delicate compassion
and wispy blond smile

a two-story
memory
both floors occupied.

The Wanting

sterile clouds
dry heat
massive love
in famine terms
praying for a rain of feeling
he concurs
with a wind that slides out of bed
the other side a forecast of frustration
there will be no drop of insemination
the earth weeps
a son evaporates
before it reaches fruition
an unaccustomed rise in pressure
perspective parents find no solace
in an omen sun
that only shines inwardly
yet shuts off the light
with hopeful fingers.

jacob erin-cilberto

your song under my skin

i still feel the blaze of your eyes
when we touched feelings
with our lips conveying
that sharing only best friends
know the tune to—

when i stroked the strands of your words
we both cried salty tears of understanding

now there is a flame in my memory
and it burns with a seared picture of you
there is darkness in the frame
your beauty a wreck from the unaccustomed roots
of a matchstick existence
snuffed out in an instance

reduced to backlash
whiplash
straightjacket retrospect

i'm in a white gown of undoing
and you are a closed casket
of captured insights

i once held in my arms

as we embraced the world together
imagining we could conquer anything at all
just never thought
for so many years

i would be playing this melody, alone
on a dim lit stage
feeling my heart spinning
like a globe off its axis.

jacob erin-cilberto

Voices in the Asylum

a spoken word
metamorphosed into an almost penned line
a whisper inked to a page
barely audible but carrying weight

enough to transform the reader
into a mood swinging carrion
maggots mourn the poet
as they munch on his multiplicity

happy homonyms find sanctity
within the breast where the heart
lies safely hidden, until that line
is almost finished

the sappy synonyms stand at attention
as the reader devours the poet's tears
and then digests them with their own
creating an organic flow of festering phonetics

driving both mad
but in that world, sanity is the stranger
ink the blood that unites the writers
and unties their bond with normalcy

we hit Dickinson's plank in reason
and we break themes like hard bread
we eat the words dry, no jam
just jammed up minds that can only

unfurl when the flags of like minds
wave in the cave of creativity
in order to keep the spoken word
surviving until it finds a page

on which to take residence
in a place others fear
to get near.

jacob erin-cilberto

Life between Two Coasters

you gave me a glass full
of trite wine
burgundy promises with cliche fingers crossed
i became sated and saturated
with a red rose rendering

of feelings awash in sipped solitary
as my blurred vision
saw something walking away from me
and the reflection in the bottom of the chandelier
was just an expensive version

of a love that made me drunk
with a stupor of stupidity
that looked you in a crystal eye.

splashed with reservations
i finally put the drink down

and retreated to the garden
to find a new bloom
a different color rose
to float in my glass
of now aged aspirations

which find themselves
ironically inebriated
as my lips
reach toward your rim of resistance.

jacob erin-cilberto

Frostbitten Roses

bitter blizzard fate
inertia's stone hearts fathom
a slow thaw awaits

Rediscovering the Elusive

love finds a way to commute
even if the distance is incalculable

love finds a way to be certain
even if life gets indeterminable

love finds us finding each other, always
even when obstacles seem immovable

and love finds us forever linked
as our hearts become more and more inseparable...

Playing a Poet with Monopoly Money

i'm a free lance poet
contact me at the number below
and i'll write you a poem for any occasion

i'll write you a love poem
a break-up poem
or a break you up poem
if you like dark humor
and don't flinch at the sarcastic punches thrown

i wield a poem like a fist
and it will knock you off your feet
make you feel incomplete
or help you to compete
for that significant other you want to
significantly impress
with your most verbose style
while i take little more than a dime
for my time

i'm a free lance poet
and all it will cost you
is small fortune
which fortunately is only make believe

because really, i don't believe a thing i write
and if you are smart you might
pass on hiring a once aspiring poet

who realizes his ink is up
and he should have retired pages ago
but never knew when to quit
so the sum of it
is this.

write your own damn words!
i am exhausted and my muse retired
long before i knew when it was time

to punch out
instead of punching at
those words that floored me years ago

with their stale jabs
roundhouse cliches—
and bleeding metaphors
no cut man can control
enough to let me continue, so

i am retracting the ad
and going home
good luck finding a ghost writer
for your ventures

i'm turning my empty pages
into play money
and drawing moustaches on poets' faces
as i pass go
then pass out from imbibing
too much liquid ego
that kept telling me
i could write.

Cyberspace Touching

whoa, hold it, please don't delete me
i am not spam,
just listen
my words are not virused or ephemerally stirred
sweet nothings.

they are something's that got into your in-box
to get your attention
you are the email i want to reply to forever
even as my fingers callous bouncing off the keys

like you bounce me off the wall,
those damn filters might cause you to miss me
might try to divert your attention to another message

but mine is sincere,
so keep it saved
and visit me often
you are the one contact
i want to feel forever on my page
locked into my favorites

you are the in-box of my life
as i look through your window
hopefully you will be looking back

and your fingers will be tapping the keys
for me.

A Wizened Wizard's Postscript

follow the screaming blacktop
the scarecrow with eyes plucked by black-winged theorists
who throw tin rants into oily confusion

the wicked witches' cauldron filled with un-symmetrical
realizations
and toto leading us because we are blind to what's really
going on
the road is endless, mindless and careless

as endeavor sings a stubborn song
and the dogs of society find themselves muzzled
against a backdrop of some motion picture fiction

there is no happy ending
the soundtrack is too slippery
and we are driving ourselves mad

with bald tires
and a tired will
that just wants to go back home

to where our hearts used to reside
when we had the courage to love
and Dorothy was not yet a glint

in a cynical director's eye.

The Harvest Thwarted

the husks are bare
the field barren brown
gasping for a last breath
as the white snow of dismal tidings
blankets the mind
with melancholy thoughts slowly trembling
toppling, parachuting to the grounded inference
that starves without the sustenance
of belief

we are crows looking for crumbs
on a landscape employed by a dreary drummer
as the beating, like that of our hearts
ebbs into an ebonic state
shortened faith lends itself to hopeless existence
and the weather never improves enough
for us to recapture the warm inception
of poems filled with expectation
of unexpected deliverance

from the cold famine that rips our emotions
from the earthen womb out of which
we are afraid to emerge.

Abstract Sorrow

i left the Green Mountains of Vermont
for the Blue Mountains of Carolina
with my Black Mountain poetry in my satchel

as i paged through a life of climbing peaks of pain
and sagacious rain
that made my heart slip and slide
precariously toward the edge

and found every crayon weeps
at one time or another
and every cliff looks inviting
at one time or another.

Rolling Over

there was a morning after
but strangely, no night before
a subtle touch in my sleep
hands dreaming of a body awakened between the lines
of the palms
in which I held your thoughts
fastened them to my heart

felt you wake with me
then opened my eyes
to the danger
of imagining
when imagination can be so deft

at lying

in the arms of a habit

my prescription ran out today
and you faded from memory
that clarity in the lens of love
a smudged nudge of perplexity

you were once my drug of choice
but the needle rusted in my vein
words became an uncomfortable fix
made me scramble in shambles
of emotion
till i got the notion to renew

and found out our relationship
was not refillable
just a one time dose
inaccessible now,
when i need you most.

jacob erin-cilberto

Brevity

simple man
simple heart
complicated love
simplicity strained
beats awkward
woman leaves
simple man
simply doesn't understand.

clutching the thought of you

skidding down a road of exile
tires bearing gifts of painful steerage
i knew you once in convertible consent
your beauty a chromed innocence

we drove each other crazily normal
and i rode your beauty into sunsets as
graveled grief
passed us like chewed up scenery

you were thrown from life much too soon
and i was strapped into my sadness
flipping over in tearful somersaults

wishing i could renew my license
to see you
just one more time

with the top down
our backs to the future
still negotiating that sudden
turn of fate

before you swerved out of my life
forever.

Imploding Voices Warn

the New York boy
found his country falling in upon itself
like an earthquake stricken high rise

the empire state's enigma
shaken to his core
as the mountains disappeared

and the water tasted stagnant
the Midwest called his name
as he spit out foul liquid
from his beleaguered brain
when pastures diluted themselves
and he deluded himself
that cows always come home
instinctively

but tremors keep happening
aftershocks of a young life
spent in concrete shoes
asphalt tension of sparse blades of grass
waiting to wither in oppressive pondering

thoughts rise higher than those buildings
he couldn't climb
as his fear of heights impedes
those steps he couldn't take

when he found the cows had gotten lost
in his mind
and the seismic deformity of his spirit
deflated the needle on his compass

until he disappeared within himself
never got to drink the potent
ale of growing old—

the New York boy
still without a country
but understanding doesn't need a flag
to identify the experience that
will follow him to his grave.

the Blues behind the Gray

sorrow spilled from your sky
i tried to catch it with rainbow gloves
but the clouds were moving disdainfully fast
causing me to drop the tears

and scratch my eyes
with swollen empathy.

The Iscariot Inference

at crucifixion crossroad
i wept a garden full of tears
you nailed my heart to an abyss
of wilted roses,
the thorns cheering as my feelings
felt the wood caress my waning spirit

you had me hanging on every word
of your proposal
and i supposed the journey
was not toward Calvary
but blue heaven

yet your Judas kiss
grounded my whims
i felt the sins of my past
repenting, repeating, rescinding

my soul
as my palms
turned red from the wounds
of missing you.

an anonymous vacancy

i'll surmise the last night
staying at the inn of borrowed time
when tomorrow will refuse to come
there will be no wake-up call
when my poet's life has taken its last sleeping pill
trudged through its last painful dream

drunk its last bouquet of words
the flowers showing telltale signs of cliched meaning
the time for one last heroic poem
even as the defecated words no longer assuage
the apocalyptic feelings

the ancient syllables of sifting sand
that no longer sift
an hour glass heart with less left than spent
you'll see my signature on the page
directly under my conclusion

even if the lines don't make much sense
you'll spy my last effort
and know all the good intent
of the weakening content

was for you.

Satirical Reservation

i think there should be nothing on my mind
in fact, i prefer it
when the tables turn
and your place setting is removed
i will eat a blank lunch of parody

knowing the evenness of the league i was in
realizing i was out of mine with you

as the saying goes "on any given day any given heart
can win over another"
but love's losing streak is just around the corner
always waiting

and all this time,
the soup was getting cold

so i'll tip my glass one more time
in your direction

smile at the empty void
sitting opposite me
and think of absolutely nothing.

Bones & Such—

you held my melting heart
in your dry, brittle hands
the bony curves of your love
a skeleton of what it once was
i felt the dust absorbed by my skin

welcomed the grave
so we could sepulcher together
enjoy infinite feasts of worms
and wine
dine in utter naivety
realize what we had been
really would decompose
&

when our rose colored glasses
mummified
we would be wrapped within each other
forever.

a Bird's Bones Reflected in a Cat's Eye

fickle, flaky feline
with your nine lives
an agenda for each
the further we go
the stealthier you move
emotions perfectly protected
while mine become a cat's treat
you gobble up my heart
with one swallow
and spit me out like a hairball

while my one life
drains into the sandy litter
of what and whom you dispose
you just lick your superficial wounds

while i become a defeathered bird
flying sidewise on my broken wing
into a tailspin
falling from the gravitational pull
of your whirlpool witted
cunningly coercive
treacherous tenders.

jacob erin-cilberto

to adverb or not to adverb, that is the question

i smilingly reviewed my poem
seemingly intrigued that it profusely used adverbs
of the vociferous kind

as i began to revise extensively
with some extremely strong resistance
from my sharply dissenting heart

i commenced quickly
to start cutting violently
and then to my utter surprise

i reread my no longer long poem
and saw clearly
i had cut it to exceedingly bleeding ribbons

and was totally left
with only an eerily mere skeleton
of my unhappily banished idea.

Bending Vows

there is a quiet kind of wind
that lifts secrets from their hiding place
and floats them past us for a glimpse
as we wonder of stationary
movement so ephemeral

and why the elastic that holds our heart in place
stretches beyond pain and back
as it leaves us no longer fitting ourselves
with the proper season of who we are

there is a quiet kind of wind
that in silence
stirs us to assay on the madness
in short clips of fashionable free verse

knowing we are not glad to be free
just an alternative to whom
we once endeavored to be...

a heart embraced
by another
creating a raucous calm
with the eloquent impunity
of a guilty poet.

There's No Funny Farm for the Likes of This

fair game Detroit crazies
burning buildings and brains hot against
the time's sentiment
not the NY Times, although some sophisticated
ivory white writer might try to position his article
in the right column,

one untouched by the flames
as he thinks he has captured the guts of the nuts
throwing TV sets through windows
and throwing windows through decades
of sparkling clean glass hate

Walter Cronkite flying through the air
his necktie unwound as the tempers
flaring, the sirens glaring
it's 1968

and we were ate up
by discolored hate
and colored fate
segregated
integrated
inundated
with mandates
and planned dates

for moving in
and moving up
forcing issues down others' already raspy throats
from the protests
and the protests
of the protests
of the protestors
with black faces and white faces
and no other places
to go,
because it was the sixties
and those years trapped us within our subconscious
without our conscious
but with deep conscience

that fair game Detroit crazies
weren't so crazy after all...
and that NY Times news blues paper

needs to print a retraction
about the action
of the crazies
who maybe just changed the world,

(at least theirs)

for at least
one moment
when the flames
were finally extinguished
even if the burning minds
were not.

His Worn out Soul

rampant dreams
street corner eyes blinking
in symphonies of relentless expectation

wakes in a dark room
some indistinct cave——
where bats actually see quite clearly

they still fly all funny
but his insides aren't laughing
and the heart just wants more sleep

wants to quit brown bagging it
and just stare into the sun
have at least one or two dreams

actually come true
even if the hot concrete
burns through the bottom of his shoes.

Boarding Pass

fly me into your friendly skies
my wings are singed
my flight pattern rejected
by another's control tower

auto pilot gets really monotonous
can't escape the doldrums of staggering heartbeats
i am constantly tripping on my own cloud of pain
yet i feel that even your rain

could make me blush again
like a painted sunset
ridges of blue-gray bordered
in red amazement

tuck me beneath your propeller breaths
sing me a wind song
and i will fasten my seat belt of trust
to your beautiful motion

as love rises into the stratosphere
higher than any heart
ever thought
it could reach.

not the "real comfortable" kind

time shrinks
like a thrice washed pair of Levis
pockets heavy with memory
cuffs scuffed from experience
color faded like ancient skin

stains, the freckles accumulated
from years of existence,
zipper a bit rusted
like the heart too often
left out in the rain
hanging on the line to dry out

emotional aches and pains
too delicate to put in the dryer
which would only shrink
time faster

it's ephemeral enough as it is
and age seems something
some of us are not wearing
too well to begin with,

but when our autumn
has its clearance sale
if the jeans still fit at all

we'll wear them one more time
before our body is given
to Goodwill...

Just an Awkward Poet's Dream

some have a green thumb for gardening
others a tin ear for music
or a Romeo void
when it comes to love
and some have a magic brush
to paint interventions of vibrant moods

but when i get near you
and try to write the words of expression
i etch a deep impression
of shadowed intent
but the poetry stutters

like a backward Shakespeare wannabe
posing plays within plays
to catch the conscience of the girl—
and still i end up
with nothing more than another
lonely soliloquy.

Before you Grew into You, there were Termites

pretty people are window shoppers
for sincerity
passing by to save a few shallow bucks
mannequins wink at each other
then laugh at the retreating footsteps

beauty in the wooden eye
a warped fantasy played like damaged records
words slipping into curt response
the scrap lumber of a new generation
birthed in
spoiled glass houses—
the stones already thrown
before the storefront's dressers
foster the guile to look past the mirror

as prim and proper platters
redo their interiors real cheap
with exactly the same deadwood.

Demolition 1

coffee table brain
in a house annihilated
a few broken chairs
nothing conventional ever sat in
thoughts lie on a carpet of worn meaning
chaotic filaments of uneven breath
abandoned teapot whistling on the stove

a bookmark notes the stoppage of a life
where much of the novel is left in doubt

cover blurbs full of denial
existence a war of words
fulfillment a tragic poem
published then torn out of the magazine
by the last barrage of bombs
dropped by critics who couldn't keep the siding
on their own conscience
and glass windows so clear
we could see them masturbating within tortured chambers
of frustration
as guilty prologues sang disparaging tunes

at an unattended funeral.

Demolition 2

a well-respected man
stiff collar
wide tie
nicely creased pants
but look in his pockets
pilfered promises
scathing words about his peers
adjunct fears
of growing broke
brokering his wealth any way he can

table his retainer
hire him out the door
his smile is dangerous
but he'll draw you in
like a child drawing stick figures in art class
he'll make you his ideal

and you the idealist
will spend the rest of your life
trying to break out of the frame
as he's hung you on his trophy wall

the picture of
a well-respected man.

Demolition 3

stay with me awhile
even if you don't mean it
sit quiet and pretend we are still friends
i want to remember you the way you were
in that frail moonlit glow
someone i thought i had gotten to know
someone i gave my heart to
when i was conspicuously naive

hiding the diary in my pocket
as i flinched from the glare
of your vacant stare
absorbing the coldness of your belligerent touch

i sort of loved you much
you became a tattoo i couldn't rub off
and reality is blindness
but i didn't want to see
i just wanted to drain your warmth
into my skin

but as i shivered away the biting wind
of your callous breezy disposition
i was stamped with deceit
like an underage slipping into the bar
illegally partaking a drink of romance

and now here we are,
sitting in silent happenstance
just an afterthought
i'm trying to maintain long enough

to have a memory
even if the moment never really happened,
i'll try to remember you
as if it did.

Demolition 4

flower power drummin'
black power fists flailing
in a lost horizon
there is movement in the beast
and years removed there is a sightless bird
winging its way into silent accord

the arthritised fingers
weakly clenched holding the note
some suicide poet who couldn't change things
with revolver words
shooting his reservoir of saintly messages
into his own head,

leaping out of the chair
the floor a comfortable net
as the hippie with the afro
played his guitar into the ground
to meet the others...

heaven scented sparrows
dictate the song
and books with dusty, untouched spines
fall silent from the shelves

back then we thought of back then
and now we still reflect on back then
when the now is written
into a sunset that seems so final

a rising is absurdity's joke
on us.

Demolition 5

family on one hand
is a clan of words
unrelated in figurative sense
yet so connected on a literal highway
that confusion is bound to speed into afterthought

and one would read the poet succinctly, as attributed
to concrete,
but that is for buildings meant to be torn down
the inner conscience is light as air yet
heavy as atmosphere when we congregate
in our misfortunate circle
and stare at each other
wishing the drive
wasn't so far.

Demolition 6

when the writing is tired
and the skeleton of meaning
hangs wearily in the shed of discontent
muddy windows convey complexities
like screaming pigs led to slaughter
words convolute the intensity
and sleepy drums symbolize
nothing
i hear the chaos from my typewriter's chamber

but expression's throat is slit
and the blood of a waning poet
shields its eyes
from a morning of latent recognition

because waking up is more painful
than the useless phrases
he conjures up to the beat
knowing he is beaten.

jacob erin-cilberto

Demolition 7

look at the vision
concentrate on what's not there
understand that conclusions drawn
in sand vary with the tide
ride a wave of caution
else you be just another castle
overwhelmed by reality's toy soldiers
and wind up as grains
of regret never to be washed away
no matter how disarming
an ocean's smile.

Demolition 8

half an arm waves
in a confederate breeze
gray skies intrude
on solemn blue rendering
daffodils unaware pose for the sun
while sons, brothers and fathers
lie like sarcophagus sheep
all in slaughtered rows,
discolored now
for in the end
the compass always points north
but the pieces can never
be put back together
exactly as they were
and death is color blind.

jacob erin-cilberto

Demolition 9

an octave lower
this
brazen hotel, no vacancy
of lust
rooms of chained melodies
poured out from
vain windows unlit
structural damage from the last
quake
withstood enough to comply again
to a ridiculous voice in the
din
of chaotic bed sheets

the chamber maid on vacation
as Holocaust cries
tear through the night
and abandonment of values
draws us all
nearer the fire.

Demolition 10

lay the bricks
mortar the martyr's dream
with a moribund mason's mix
rebirth is in stacked blocks of hope
let the sleeping termites tend to their would's
strength is in the could's
and we could build our house from past pain
make it so strong the present will close its shutters
light our fire from within
burn the candles into patterns on walls of plastered faith

we can build it
it will come
and love will tile the roof, sacrificing us
with the warmth of a detachedly
thatched sun.

Demolition 11

cry me a river?
i can't, sorry

only have a pond left
and it has been drying up for years
the life within floating listlessly to the surface
reflection—— a maze of grief
murky images of mistakes
eddies of incongruities swirling in my mind
vanishing
into cold comfortable muddy bottom

i am looking up
with weary eyes
the ache no longer current
the current no longer a movement

i am still, not a ripple
of interest left
for you,

not a tear to shed
since i shed my love
like an unbaited hook.

courting the heat

you were my little transistor heartthrob—-
played your song in my ear—
a top 40 kiss beating against my chest

as i danced out of my adolescence
tapping the feet of my youth
against the dashboard of desire

when being driven out of our minds
by another's body of evidence
was only a misdemeanor.

jacob erin-cilberto

The Gospel according to Those who Can Afford it (Everything's Cool)

simple man
poorer by day
suicidal by night
the blade invites
the green refuses
his pastures keep getting smaller
God bless the rich aristo-cat- the cool-cat
who gets richer on the simple man's
conscience
God bless the skyscrapers with suits
God bless the planes who find idle
fingers sitting at desks
in the name of God
the simple man finds his world
simply shallower with each swallow
each breath of religion
of poverty
of books that profess
the meek shall inherit the earth,

God bless the politicians who rule for the majority
of their own likeness
padding accounts on account it is how God intends
as they spend their kindness
with their own kind,
God bless the drunk in the alley
holding mass among the trash can pews
for the few

with strength enough to cross themselves
and put their hands together, clasped in prayer
and gratitude for the buck or two
to spend on a sandwich and a bottle
God bless those who carry peace signs from the sixties
but have become insulated yuppies
shielded from the cause—
cause it ain't there no more—

God bless the hate
God bless the apathy—
God bless the souls on Sunday
who close their eyes
and take communion
and offer up a tear or two
for those who can't even afford to cry

don't worry, God will make it all better
even if we do nothing,
God bless the inert beings who pretend a country is great—
when its fate
is a plane heading for a monument
that will be filled with the names
of those who almost fought equality
who almost fought for justice for all
who almost lifted a finger, except to change the remote

remote hands, remote minds, remote intentions
God bless America
God bless the simple man—
simple will find sanctuary in the end
but that church door will be closed
to the rest,

may they rest in peace.

There was a Cause once, before the 45's got Flip-sided

now there's a chaotic peace
next door to the sixties i used to know
but now i am sixty-something
trying to taste a new beat
wanting the body parts to stop inverting
in covert moves, rusting hinges
i am a door squeaking with uselessness

i used to mean something
but at sixty-something
love is but a blush
passion is a passing subway
making a little noise
but staying out of sight

and she just stares with those slight tears
and puzzled expression
at the bones of the man beside her

and then goes back to her book,
while he plays music in his mind
doing the Jimmy Page air guitar
bashing his instrument against his frustration

he used to play, he imagines to himself
and she used to stop and listen
before she turned off her reading lamp
and thought back to when that subway was a submarine

he was the captain
and she couldn't wait to submerge herself
in his "Sea of Love."

safe from the shrapnel

i sat in an alleyway
of "till death do us part"
drinking moonshine substitute
because my own moon let me down
after it led me down the aisle of white

and words now beg for handouts
after ones said from the mass missal
became mass missiles of anger and
resentment
before we ran into the embankment
of entrapment

fenders dented by offending mishaps
in what was once a happy cruise
with nothing to lose...

promises feel very cold now
as the north winds chap my hands
and my chapped heart
longs for warmth

i grip the bottle tighter
take another swig of sauntering backwards in time
invite the clouds to share tears
for the seemingly lost years

as i meander down the block
"honor, love and cherish"
tucked safely under a
full metal jacket.

I thought you were a poet, once

i read you
your words seemed inflated
your cheeks flushed
the sentences stiff and uncolored
your eyes told lies
your poems kept secrets
i read you
wasn't a book i couldn't put down
but you put words down on a page
and they seemed to lie flat
airy but non-committal
like you hoped for a purpose
and thought it would drop into your poems
a nonplussed theme
a thesis statement curt and raging
like the bated breath that spewed from your mouth
unceremoniously
when you spoke in wretched parables
with no hidden meanings
no surface meanings

and no reason
except to defer your love
into poems
i read you
and you seemed loveless
the poems like vagrants inhabiting a building
with no heat,
i am cold now
the candle is nearly flickered out
chances are
the book of you is closed
i know you will keep writing
like a shark in shallow water
carnivorously filling your stomach
with unsuspecting, stolen words
but i'm smart enough to walk the beach
i like sand between my pages
not current that chills the truth
till the windows frost over.

jacob erin-cilberto

Stuck in the Dogma of the Dogma

i stumbled across a tenet
tried to believe in Jesus
and sin and forgiveness—
and resurrections
and souls transcending earth
to live in another place

but the tenet turned into tenement halls
and writing on the walls that confused me
so i found my own wall
wrote something on it
and then tried to believe
in myself.

the man at the corner of his life

a hand reaches out
a car goes by
a cardboard sign waves like a weak flag
in a disconcerting wind

the stomach talks
bad words,
angry words
belching sounds, hungry sounds

the cardboard wilts in the rain
the drops meld with tears
the hand becomes weaker
barely outstretched

one meal away from comfort
one dollar away from dignity
one bottle away from forgetting
one medley of songs burning inside his head

a poor man's recording
the record spinning wearily
the lettered lyrics on the cardboard
run in the rain

if only he still had the energy to
he'd run from this life
waving his white flag
in a disconcerting wind.

jacob erin-cilberto

Hungry in the Stairwell of Lost Faith

a brooklyn stone's throw
from a bent bronx fabric of
skyscraper sinewy shadows

city lamp lights casting bleak
shades upon a lonely borough
where the hearts cry nightly

on forsaken streets
those long forgotten souls
seeking a taste of redemption

not a handout
but a hand to hold
a heart beating next to theirs

in rhythm with the subway music
heard down below, in that purgatory
of mindless melody

caught in between, where
the stone lands upon a wilderness
filled with concrete trees

that really don't grow in brooklyn
although fable plants the seed
the needy never really find that shade of contentment

that elevator to take them up to heaven
or the 100th floor
which ever comes first by way

of the swollen night's transit.

jacob erin-cilberto

Judgement's Song

demonstrative hands
tired palms
fingers bleeding through the air
arguing with filaments of dusty preaching
the mouth moves
the hands lip synch the dance

expression in the knuckles
as the voice punches sound
and the silent fingers
curl and fade and spar
like subtitles
fighting to be heard

words find their voice
in motion
demonstrative hands
question with movement
a ringside seat to thoughts
expressed and impressed

like jabs in the gut
that knock us down
with their power
and send us reeling to the floor
like a partner
spun dizzy,
till the music's over.

the Plagiarist

i seem to be out of words
so maybe i'll just borrow some of yours
the muse packed up and moved out
now my vacant brain feels like a
structure of brittle bone
that can no longer bend toward shared theme

the other side of creativity
is like an empty side of the bed
and what used to seem
a lifelong partner
is just a memory of misshaped ideas

so now it might still be my tone
my ruptured structure
but the empty house
in which resides my poetic solitude
still needs to be pretend

so if you recognize my companion
and she looks a bit like your significant other
i am only stealing a few connotative kisses, a little word
holding
and bit of stanza-ed serenity
to call my own,

just until my elegiac heart
can heal enough
to find its own voice
once again.

jacob erin-cilberto

Three Senryu Goodbye

simple tears fall from
complicated love affairs
as her patience wanes

~~~~~~~~~~~~~~~~~

lipstick inference
nothing close to her color
more his shade of red

~~~~~~~~~~~~~~~~~

bags packed with regret
zips up the last of her love
picks up bus schedule

~~~~~~~~~~~~~~~~~

Senryu on the Menu

Breakfast

sunny side up smile
she serves him pain over easy
he knows he is toast

~~~~~~~~~~~

Lunch

a chilled interest
she invites his waning heart
to share her cold cuts

~~~~~~~~~~~

Dinner

he awaits entree
she dashes away like salt
his spice of life, gone

~~~~~~~~~~~

Midnight Snack

he dreams fervently
heart aches for some nourishment
moonlit memories

a truism about the catechism of lust (acrostically speaking)

amazing woman contours my vision

libido calling, mind a smatter of bad intentions

i can't focus clearly on morality's body, hers is in the way

verisimilitude—like my eyes are bloodshot with truth serum

every line in her whimsical smile, i have written before—

and will write again.

the old days march into the new days

standing at attention
in the photo on the wall of memory
uniform creased with perfection's hand
smile crisp and penetrating
features dissolved into black and white
the camera angle just right
to show that total commitment to the shoot

the one that happens overseas
somewhere far away,
captured in a moment when the sun
is in perfect formation
when fears are shaded away
behind the frame of reference
for a soldier dressed to kill—
because he has to,

i stare into the abyss of his eyes
and wonder their reflection
when he was still alive,
for now he only stands at attention
on a vertical wall,
while his body is a horizontal symbol
which lies in a state of question

asking if the cause
was worth the film
it took to capture that moment.

How is the View from up There?

you are a model of incoherency
babble talk,
scuttlebutt logic
contradictions galore
your eyes give you away
as your tongue lashes lavishly, linguistically
lowering the ego of others
from an engaging river heroically taming a sea
to a small stream of sensitivity
losing its momentum,
the words drying up even as they flow

the fine line of semantic simpatico
you destroy as you cross
the bridges you burn in guise
of being prominent and worldly in your poetic stance

i've read the likes of you before
seen the ruin of ethics
absorbed in the theme of theoretical amazement
you confound us with

you are an acrobat on your own pretentious high wire
with a net one metric foot below,
as we all hold our breath

waiting for your fall,
hoping the mesh is weak enough
to allow you to plummet
(within your own resounding rhetoric)

to your deathly conundrum
as the beat of your catastrophic connotation
finds harsh ending
when you are swallowed up
pen and all...
in the cold ground of utterance.

the old gardener's prayer

happy corrosion
bits of my heart curdling
like old lactate
bubbling red
flowers bowing to your beauty
intrepid interest
paying dividends of love

i would gladly expire in your presence
erosion's empathy by my side
likening itself
to the sour sips
i embrace
just as i do my rambunctious rose

you'll find me in your garden
way past my due date.

jacob erin-cilberto

jacob erin-cilberto,
originally from Bronx, NY,
now resides in
Carbondale, Illinois.
erin-cilberto has been
writing and publishing
poetry since 1970. He
currently teaches at John
A. Logan and Shawnee
Community colleges in Southern Illinois.

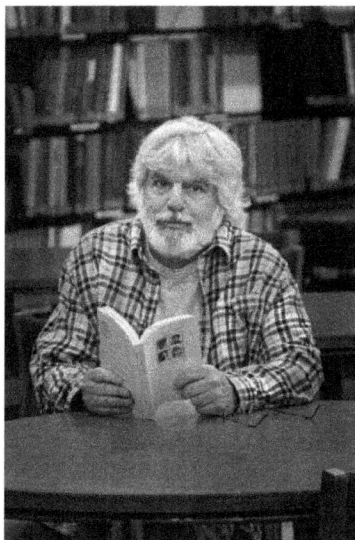

His work has appeared in numerous small magazines and
journals including: Café Review, Skyline Magazine, Hudson
View, Wind Journal, Pegasus, Parnassus and others. erin-
cilberto also writes reviews of poetry books for Chiron
Review, Skyline Review, Birchbrook Press and others. He has
reviewed books by B.Z Niditch, Michael Miller, Barry
Wallenstein, Marcus Rome, musician Tom MacLear and
others. His previous three books *an Abstract Waltz, Used
Lanterns and Intersection Blues* are available through Water
Forest Press. His books are also available on Barnes and
Noble.com and Amazon.com as well as Goodreads. erin-
cilberto has been nominated for a Pushcart Prize in Poetry
in 2006-2007-2008 and again in 2010. He teaches poetry
workshops for Heartland Writers Guild, Southern Illinois
Writers Guild and Union County Writers Guild.

www.ingramcontent.com/pod-product-compliance
Lightning Source LLC
Chambersburg PA
CBHW071236090426
42736CB00014B/3099

* 9 7 8 0 6 9 2 4 0 9 1 8 3 *